What We Still Don't Know

poems by

Dawn Paul

Finishing Line Press
Georgetown, Kentucky

What We Still Don't Know

Copyright © 2019 by Dawn Paul
ISBN 978-1-64662-080-7 First Edition
All rights reserved under International and Pan-American Copyright Conventions. No part of this book may be reproduced in any manner whatsoever without written permission from the publisher, except in the case of brief quotations embodied in critical articles and reviews.

ACKNOWLEDGMENTS

My thanks to Morgan Talty (Editor-in-Chief) and the editorial team at *Stonecoast Review* at University of Southern Maine who first published "Bradypus."

I am indebted to Wilfrid Blunt for information on Linnaeus from his excellent book, *Linnaeus: The Compleat Naturalist*.

Thank you to my North Shore writing community, always there with honesty and care: Cindy Veach, Colleen Michaels, Danielle Jones, Elisabeth Horowitz, January O'Neil, J.D. Scrimgeour, Jennifer Jean, Jennifer Martelli, Kathleen Aguero, Kevin Carey and M.P. Carver.

With gratitude to Moira Linehan for our years of reading each other's writing and especially for this collection of poems.

Love and thanks to Marilyn McCrory, who makes everything possible.

Publisher: Leah Maines
Editor: Christen Kincaid
Cover Art: Public Domain image, JJ Audubon
Author Photo: Marilyn Humphries, humphriesphotography.com
Cover Design: Elizabeth Maines McCleavy

Printed in the USA on acid-free paper.
Order online: www.finishinglinepress.com
also available on amazon.com

Author inquiries and mail orders:
Finishing Line Press
P. O. Box 1626
Georgetown, Kentucky 40324
U. S. A.

Table of Contents

The Second Adam 1

Kingdoms 2

Young Carl Scandalizes the Botanists 3

The Lappmark Adventure 4

My Dearest Peter 6

Binomial Nomenclature 7

Bradypus 8

Order Anthropomorpha—The Primates 9

"He illumines" 10

Lectotype 11

Yet, But 12

Homo monstrosus 13

Pelecanus occidentalis 14

Cryptids 15

A Just Proportion 16

Bottom Line Zero 17

The Most Trafficked Animal in the World 18

Linnaea borealis 19

The Elisabeth Linnaeus Phenomenon 20

Watching the Floral Clock 21

Instructions for Burial 23

The Second Adam

He bestowed a name on every living thing in his world.
Twenty-thousand animals alone. And all the plants.
"God created. Linnaeus organized," he said modestly.
In his day, they called him The Second Adam,
as he roamed, collected, ordered and named.
His name on the tongue of every educated man.
Whose mother had despaired of his future,
a young failure good for nothing but botany.
She had planned on a more sacred vocation.
Instead, he worshipped in meadows and at rough edges of fields,
kneeling, picking, sniffing, "completely stunned
by the incredible resourcefulness of the Creator."

The Romantics derided
"this naturalist with his urge to classify,"
who, Wordsworth wrote, was
"…a fingering slave
One that would peep and botanize
Upon his mother's grave…"
He may well have stroked that grass,
greeting the plants he knew
with more passion and attention
than he gave to her mourners.
A botany student of twenty-six,
completely stunned at her loss.

Kingdoms

I picture Linnaeus cleaving the living world in two:

Plants   Animals

Then a gentle sorting:

barley	elephant
rubber tree	hoptoads
duckweed	lampreys
roses	larks
foxglove	badgers
fennel	butterflies

Kingdoms without kings:
green moss by the brook
tucked in with mighty oaks,
treacherous toadstools
under a bower of grapes.

The animals? No Noah's ark, with its couples
by invitation only. But a teeming world of
lions, lambs, clams and eagles,
teal, hedgehogs,
haddock and grouse.
The heron that hunts the frog that hunts the fly.

That first rough cut, that separated Eve from the apple,
puts me in, not with the morning glory
that knows to climb the gatepost to catch the early sun,
but with the blind grubs that curl in its roots.

Young Carl Scandalizes the Botanists

To classify a flower, Linnaeus would have you
gently part its petals, brushing the golden pollen
on the stamens, the husbands in his marriages
among the flowering plants.
Count the stamens.
Two? The flower belongs to the Class *Diandria*,
"Two husbands in the same marriage."
Counting, counting, twenty and still counting? *Polyandria*,
"twenty males or more in the same bed with the female,"
a state of affairs enjoyed by the poppy and the linden.
And those plants whose flowery parts you search for in vain?
Like the softly rounded mosses or pale delicate cups of mushrooms?
Linnaeus prepared a Class for these as well:
Cryptogamia, "hidden marriage."

Now, to place the flower in its proper taxonomical Order,
push the husbands aside to expose
the wives with their sticky pistils. Count them.
Monogynia, for one, *digynia* for two, *trigynia* for three
and on and on and on.

Nature, however, does not bend itself to systems.
There are those flowers who would queer his tidy marriages.
Some verbena have two stamens, some have four.
Yet Linnaeus placed them all in the Class *Diandria*, two,
permitting double entendres, but not double entries.

An adolescent when he created his lively taxonomy, Linnaeus later said
the "remarkable office of the stamens and pistils enticed my mind,
to inquire what Nature had concealed in them."
Then he entered the delights of his flower beds,
counting and counting.

The Lappmark Adventure
from Linnaeus's Journal of Notes and Drawings

It began with "an incredible longing" to see the mountains.
Then, a request to the Swedish Royal Society of Science for 600 copper dalers for a four months' journey of 1600 miles that would—he stated—require a Swede, young and active, very fit, very tough, and a bachelor. Trained in medicine and natural history. Able to draw. In short, himself.
They gave him only 400.
His father gave his blessing: "If you are confident that this journey will advance your career, then ask God for guidance and help. He is everywhere, even among the wildest fells. Trust in Him. My prayers go with you."
So the journey began. "In my bag I carried this journal...a shirt...a gauze veil to protect me from midges...a stock of sheets of paper to press plants between...my Flora Uplandica book."

"I was twenty-five years old, all but about half a day."

"Now the whole world laughs and sings...Linnaea borealis! grows abundantly...the sweet lark sang no more...the song-thrush welcomed us to the forest...in this desolate wilderness I began to feel very lonely and longed for a companion...a collar made of birch bark pinned around the neck as protection from the rain."

Laplanders offered hospitality. "The Lapps lie stark naked, with only reindeer-skin coverlets...from her chest, which was like the skin of a frog, were suspended a pair of long limp brown dugs...It tasted good and strong, but my appetite was spoiled by the way the spoon was cleaned; the husband took water into his mouth and spat upon the spoon." His final appraisal of his hosts: "The Lapps live free of worry, strife and discord, without knowing what envy is..."

A pen and ink sketch: a baby Lapp lashed in its cradle

"...pink-flowered Andromeda at the height of its beauty...raw fish, whose mouths were full of worms, and the sight took away my appetite...the underjaw of a horse, having six fore-teeth, much worn and blunted, two canine teeth, and at a certain distance from the latter twelve grinders, six on each side...rain, fog, thunder, lightning... mosses and lichens..."

More sketches: an owl, a cranefly with delicate crumpled legs, lumpy mountains

"...holes in reindeer hides are caused by the larvae of a species of gadfly...a smoky hut, ventilated only by holes in the roof...and when I ascended the mountains, I knew neither if I was in Africa nor Asia since the soil, situation and plants were entirely unfamiliar...I climbed to the highest point to see the midnight sun."

"I sat down to collect and describe plants so that time was completely forgotten."

For the Society's 400 dalers, he gave them five months of rough living, three thousand miles, and two hundred observations on the natural history of Lapland. And a book of plant studies, *Flora Lapponica*, in which he admits to being "glad, very glad indeed, to have the comforts of civilization again."
"Recollections of Lapland," a final sketch: a Lapp tent with reindeer, a Lapp carrying his boat over his head, mountains upon mountains, the sun with a baleful face, rays of light shooting outward.

He was never to make such a journey ever again.

My Dearest Peter

I have kept our pledge.
Your book, your beautiful *Ichthyologia*,
will be published this month in Leyden.
I hope it makes your fame
as my botany books have made mine.
Who would have known when we made that pledge,
ragged students in Sweden, sent by our parents
to become clergymen, but finding a different kind of worship,
that chance would bring us together again three years later
in Amsterdam? I remember that long night
when I brought you my new botany manuscript
and you insisted on reading what you had written
of your fishes. How alike we were, our minds bent
on classification! You with your minute details
of scale and fin, me with my petals and pistils!
Now I am sorry about that night. I was so exhausted.
The hour so late, the lamp dimming.
You had been living such a lonely life, even for you,
nothing but work and sleep.
But you kept me so long, so unendurably long.
Had I known then that I would be the one left
to honor our pledge that the survivor
would give to the world the observations of the other.
I can never love Amsterdam, only think of the canal
where just a few nights later you stumbled and drowned
(oh, I can imagine the darkness, the late hour, your mind
whirling with fishes).
I have named a flower for you, one of the Umbrelliferae,
for I know you always loved them: *Artedia*

Peter Artedi, author of *Ichthyologia—The Natural History of Fishes*, is known today as the Father of Ichthyology.
Parts of this poem are from the writings of Carl Linnaeus, who published Artedi's book in 1738.

Binomial Nomenclature
Carl for the Swedish king, Linné for the lime tree

From the jumble-box of mother tongues,
all those boat and slipper shells—*Crepidula*.
Beach-strewn winged kelp, dapper-locks, honey ware—*Alaria*.
Even the ancient gods weren't spared:
Venus's girdle, the comb jelly *Cestum veneris*
and Neptune's shaving brush, the algae *Penicillis*.
Felis clarifies cats who are not cats,
like the polecat *Mephitis mephitis*, Latin for stench,
or *Martes pennanti*, who is not a fisher-cat, but a weasel.
Felis concolor lets us be specific when being chased
by a mountain lion, catamount, cougar,
wildcat, panther, puma.
Canis keeps the dogs inside and out,
familiaris by the fire, *lupus* howling at the door.

Dignified *Buxbaumia* is bug-on-a-stick moss,
and those lovely sisters of the sea, *Doris*, *Mya* and *Daphnia*?
Sea slugs, clams and water fleas.
Fregata, the frigate bird, shows roots in Romance languages.
Note chewy incisors in *Incisitermes*, the dry-wood termite,
the horse in *Equisetum*, the horsetail rush.
Others have entered common use, *Magnolia* and *Digitalis*,
and there's little house *Mus*, and big cousin *Rattus*.
Red cedars are *Juniperus*, *Cedrus* is a cedar,
long-necked *Cygnus* with her train of little cygnets.
The shipworm *Teredo* sinks a ship like a torpedo,
and *Saccharum* distills to sweet-fire rum.
Camelus with one hump or two.
Labyrinthula, the slime net, makes perfect sense,
while *Wolffia*, meek duckweed, makes no sense at all.
Tulipa and *Yucca* make it easy to guess,
Gorilla gorilla makes it obvious.

Bradypus
> *(Latin "slow of foot")*

Look at the face of a sloth:
round red eyes,
protruding leathery snout,
stingy, lipless mouth.
Fur swept back from the brooding forehead
in a kind of pompadour that extends the length
of its body. So slow,
it seems to ooze dream-like from branch to branch,
hooking a three-fingered claw, reaching perpetually
caught between sleeping and waking.

What was Linnaeus thinking, to place *Bradypus*
in the Order Anthropomorpha, the man-like apes?
Perhaps he had seen it swim, which it does quite well,
a sinuous stroke and glide.
Or he saw something human in those long, slim arms,
supplication or purpose…or its very slowness gave it an air
of deliberation, contemplation.

In any event, the sloth's invitation to join us was rescinded.
By the next edition of Linnaeus's taxonomy, *Bradypus* was banished
by a new rule demanding five digits on each hand.

Order Anthropomorpha-The Primates

> *Each taxonomy is a theory about the creatures it classifies.*
> —Stephen J. Gould

Observe: two legs, two arms, a spine in the upright position, a head upon a neck.
We could share a wardrobe. Five toes on flat, flexible feet. And shoes!
An ear on each side of that head. Headphones, earmuffs.
Forward-facing eyes. Sunglasses, binoculars.
A mouth that can frown, grin, pout. Or smoke a cigarette.
And those clever hands, those thumbs. That can hold a stick, a pen, let us hitchhike
or wear an outfielder's mitt.
You've seen them in videos: probing termite mounds with twigs, using touch screens,
making lethal raids on neighbors.
So easy to see our common ancestor climbing down from the trees to the savannah,
and eventually, the world.
Seventy-four years before Charles Darwin was born,
one-hundred and twenty-four years before *The Origin of Species*,
despite huffy protestations from his fellow Christian biologists,
Linnaeus, too, observed them. And us, perhaps late at night
at a tavern in Stockholm.

"He illumines"
> *motto on a silver medal struck in honor of Linnaeus, 1747*

He once buried his silk purse, heavy with a hundred ducats,
to prove the divining rod was superstitious nonsense.
It was said he would have classified the angels
had he observable knowledge of them.
But as he did not, angels remained in Heaven,
out of his rational reach.

Here on Earth, he sub-divided *Homo sapiens* into four *taxa*,
classified not by custom, culture or land of origin,
but by the observable trait of skin color:
Americanus, Asiaticus, Africanus, Europeaeus.

Later, he added these observations to his famous taxonomy:
Americanus, "reddish, choleric, and erect; hair black... wide nostrils...
obstinate, merry, free... regulated by customs."
Asiaticus, "sallow, melancholy, stiff; hair black, dark eyes... severe,
haughty, avaricious... ruled by opinions."
Africanus, "black, phlegmatic... hair black, frizzled... nose flat; lips
tumid; women without shame, they lactate profusely; crafty, indolent,
negligent... governed by caprice."
Europeaeus, "white, sanguine, muscular... eyes blue, gentle... inventive...
governed by laws."

This Swedish botanist and lecturer, toiling away in Uppsala,
in the midst of the Enlightenment.

Lectotype

For each species, one specimen
must be chosen to step forward,
to say, I am the one, I represent all of my kind.
Linnaeus meticulously collected, described, sorted, archived,
selected one for each species he named.

For Homo sapiens, he could have plucked anyone on earth,
gone to the New World for an Americanus rubescens,
or the Dark Continent for an Africanus niger,
or the Orient for Asiaticus fufeus.
But Carolus Linnaeus, Europaeus albus,
easily available for study in Sweden,
would do as well as any of us.

Yet, But

Hard-nosed realist, Carl Linnaeus,
fingered the famed Hydra of Hamburg
seven heads, teeth and claws,
found fraud in the stitches that mixed
snakeskin, weasel paws, mammalian stuffing.

Yet, what to do with those other creatures,
sailors' tales from far-off places?
Phoenix, Dragon, Unicorn
hodge-podged as Hamburg's Hydra.
Scales, wings, beaks, tails,
the Manticore's human face with blue eyes.

Linnaeus let them roam remote parts of the globe.
But not unclassified.
At the heart of his omnibus chart Regnum Animale
he penned them in: Paradoxa

Homo monstrosus
> *"wild and monstrous humans, unknown groups, and more or less abnormal people"* —*Systema Naturae, 10th edition*

The cities of Europe will not keep them.
Lawless, God-less, comfortless.
Human nonetheless.
Though driven off
with fire and rock,
the wretches
will not leave us,
want to cleave to us,
will not slink or lumber away.
In wilderness not content
they come to join us.
Filthy hands reaching
eyes beseeching
"let me be beside you."
He gave even them a place.
Separate, but within.

Pelecanus occidentalis
   (named by Linnaeus in 1758)

'Tis true, it's a great white thing, feet yellow as the Swedish flag.
I've seen them coasting above the waves—he makes
a lofting motion with a hand missing thumb and index—
tight like soldiers on parade. One will peel off, pull in its wings,
drop like a stone! The strangest thing of it—he leans in, beer fumes
come off him strong enough to singe his listener's nose hairs—
is the mouth, big as a drawbridge. Comes up out of the water, that
mouth's puffed out like a Spanish wine sack, chockful of fish.
When it can't find fish, it stabs its own thigh with its beak,
feeds the young with fresh flowing blood.
He swears to it, this drink-addled, half-blind sailor,
in a city tavern on a winter night in 1734.

Linnaeus scoffs. The sailor, using his maimed hand,
slides his cup across the table with a sly, wet smile.
Another dram, he'll tell another tale. Sea serpents, unicorns,
whatever his listener wants to hear.
The prudent scientist pushes back his chair,
draws his cloak around his shoulders.
Enough foolishness for a night.
Outside, the wind has come up. The sound of his boot heels
on the frozen streets of Uppsala ring out in the silence.
The sky is a confusion of stars, obscured then revealed
as storm clouds billow and swirl.
He feels the creature pull at him, a huge spectral bird
drifting down the edge of a new continent.
He turns in at his gate, whispers to the dark,
Who knows what we still don't know?

Cryptids

> *"those creatures never seen by dint of their own secrecy"*
> —Linnaeus, Systema Naturae, 10th edition

Islands have stories of little people.
Sneaky, malevolent, wielding the power
of the powerless, to trick, to ruin.
Sour the milk, hide the hammer,
curse the newborn child.
A shadow at dawn,
slipping out of the cowshed,
or tiny feet heard tapping
across the hearth late at night.
Ireland's Leprechauns, Hawaii's Menehune,
the Trow of the Orkney Islands.
Catch one and make it tell its secrets.

Then there is *Homo floresiensis*, Lectotype LB1:
a woman thirty-years-old, three feet tall.
Her bones found in Liang Bua cave,
50,000 years after she died.
Not a small individual, but a new species,
evolved, as island animals sometimes do,
to become smaller.
She and her species named
for the island of Flores, Indonesia,
where people still speak of the Ebu Gogo,
small, hairy cave-dwellers,
who, they claim, kidnapped children, stole food.
Who, they say, once killed a human baby.
For this, they were hunted down in the rainforest.
Now, people say, they are all gone.

A Just Proportion

> *"...it seems that [God's] Providence not only aimed at sustaining, but also keeping a just proportion amongst all the species; and so prevent any one of them increasing too much, to the detriment of men, and other animals."*
> —Linnaeus, Oeconomia naturae (The Economy of Nature) 1775

In his profound faith and love of order
he accepted a natural world
reduced to an accountant's ledger.
Failed to discern in wilderness
God's game of pick-up-sticks
remove one and all will shift:

sea otters seemingly ∞

+ hunters and fur traders (rapacious) ≥ sea otters =
    < sea otters (eaters of sea urchins) ∴
    sea urchins (burgeoning) ≥ kelp (eaten) =
Δ kelp = Steller's sea cows (starving) ∴

∑ Steller's sea cows = 0

Bottom Line Zero

Steller's sea cow
Jamaican monkey
Reunion shelduck
Rodrigues owl
lesser Antillean macaw
Reunion ibis
Mauritius grey parrot
Tahiti sandpiper
Sardinian pika
Society (Islands) parakeet
white-winged sandpiper
Rodrigues solitaire…

…all in his lifetime.

The Most Trafficked Animal in the World*

Linnaeus named the pangolin *Manis*,
"spirits of the dead."
Nocturnal and solitary,
the size of a cat,
scaly and narrow-faced, like an anteater
in the armor of King Arthur's knights.
Sashaying through the night,
like a walking artichoke or a dragon,
front paws held up as if in prayer.
In Indonesian, *manis* means sweet.
Truly *sui generis*.
God the Creator on an impish day.

How many of you did it take to make
three tons of your scales found stuffed into bags
hidden in, of all places,
an Ivory Coast elementary school?
Waiting to be shipped to China,
$80,000 worth of worthless cures for cancer.
Spirits of the dead, did they sell your meat, too?
A million of you trafficked in the last ten years.
You are gone from Asia, dwindling in Africa.
How soon will you be your name?

*International Union for the Conservation of Nature, 20 April 2017

Linnaea borealis

Twin flower—a duo of goblet-shaped blooms top the stalk,
each leaf with a double, clinging opposite.
Abundant and cheerful, a robust wildflower
of tundra and mountain tops.
A sturdy stem crowns his family coat of arms.
Drawn in his journals,
described in his books,
painted on a porcelain tea set
carried all the way from China.
Specimens pressed in paper,
engraved on a dainty set of glasses,
carved by his own hands
on the handle of his walking stick.
In his favorite portrait, he stands proudly,
young and almost handsome in rough Laplander garb,
holding a sprig of its pink blossoms in his right hand.
He described it as "lowly, insignificant, disregarded,
flowering but for a brief space.." named, he wrote
(with false modesty, his biographers claim),
"from Linnaeus who resembles it."

The Elisabeth Linnaeus Phenomenon

She knows the plants in her father's garden at Hammarby,
knows that when she joins him on his botanical rambles,
he cannot help himself from naming, explaining.
Though she is only a daughter.
A sideways kind of learning. The straight-forward Latin and Greek,
her father's leather-bound volumes, forbidden to her.

So when she sees it at dusk the first time,
she does not believe her eyes—almost.
But she knows she has her father's keen sight,
observes as the petals of the Indian cresses seem to catch fire,
watches their edges blaze each summer evening.
When night falls, what she calls her "flashing flowers" go dark.
She sees enough, this level-headed Swedish girl,
to know that this phenomenon is real, writes a paper
for the Royal Swedish Academy of Science,
"Concerning the Flickering of the Indian Cress."
It is 1762. Elisabeth is only nineteen.
What else will the world hold
for her?

Later, Goethe will observe flashing flowers in his own garden.
The Romantic poets, enamored of electricity, will celebrate her
wondrous phenomenon, "*...a fair electric flame...*"
And she who observed this marvel first?
Dead in twenty years' time at Hammarby,
an army officer's wife, mother of two children.
Her name given by the Academy to a flash, a spark,
seen briefly at dusk.

Watching the Floral Clock

In the dream you cannot sleep.
You turn to check the alarm clock, then remember: time is reckoned
by Linnaeus's Floral Clock, the opening and closing of flowers.
So you step out into the garden, soil cool under your bare feet.
The moon is high overhead, yellow Goat's-Beard in bloom. 3 AM.
Now you know why the flower's other name is Jack-Go-To-Bed-At-
    Noon.
You must get back to sleep.

Morning! Bright yellow Hawkweed tells you it's early, 6 AM.
You are eager to start the day. Coffee, fresh peach muffins.
The news reports a major peace treaty, to be signed when the black
cherries are ripe.
Russia will release all dissidents, right before the wheat harvest.
You set out a bowl of milk for the half-wild cat that slinks out from
under the shed,
see the blue center of Scarlet Pimpernel. 8 o'clock already.
You work in the garden, stop for a mid-morning cup of iced mint tea
when the Star-hawkbit closes at 10. When the Marsh Sow-thistle closes,
each of its blossoms lasting only one day, it's lunchtime.
You pick new greens and an early tomato for a salad.

White Waterlilies in the garden pool pull in their petals,
and you feel an ache in your arms and legs. You didn't notice
the Marigolds closing, missed your afternoon break.
Much too busy with onions and carrots to thin and weed,
compost to turn and screen.
Hurry or you'll be late. Next thing you know,
Daylilies will shrivel into themselves,
your dinner guests will be at the gate.
They said they'd be here
when the Iceland Poppies close.

You check the Poppies, petals still papery,
so you still have plenty of time.

But what is that noise,
mechanical, shrill,
like a colossal locust
has landed in your garden—

Instructions for Burial

What would you leave,
if you left nothing undone?

Could you sit at rest, as old Linnaeus sat
having written his seventy-odd books?

Content in his garden in solitude,
the sun on his beloved plants.

An old cart horse, he called himself,
worn out with work, not sixty-five years.

Plants in the royal gardens of England and France
bore names he gave them.

His students travelled the globe,
brought him gifts of strange flora and fauna.

Even King Gustav III came to visit,
left his escort sitting horseback in the rain.

When unsteady, his health broken,
still he spoke with strength of heathers and heaths.

Physician, zoologist, taxonomer, yet it was Prince of Botanists
he wished carved on his gravestone

and left instructions for his burial—*unshaven, unwashed, unclothed, wrapped only in a sheet*—to hasten his return to dirt.

Dawn Paul's interest in 18th century botanist and taxonomer Carl Linnaeus began with her interest in natural history and grew as she researched his remarkable life, contradictory attitudes, and the scientific world of his times. Paul teaches writing and interdisciplinary studies at Montserrat College of Art and has taught poetry workshops at festivals, art/writing centers, and wildlife sanctuaries.

Her poems have been published in the nature and place anthologies *Birdsong, The Absence of Something Specified (Drought)* and the *Old Frog Pond Farm Chapbook*. They have also been published in journals including *Stonecoast Review, Paterson Literary Review, Comstock Review, Contemporary Haibun* and *Naugatuck River Review*.

She has an MFA from Goddard College and has been a recipient of residencies at the Vermont Studio Center, the Ragdale Foundation, the Spring Creek Project and Friday Harbor Marine Laboratories. She kayaks, backpacks, skis and bikes in New England.

www.ingramcontent.com/pod-product-compliance
Lightning Source LLC
LaVergne TN
LVHW040118080426
835507LV00041B/1775